Kids and Kites K-3

Frank Heyman

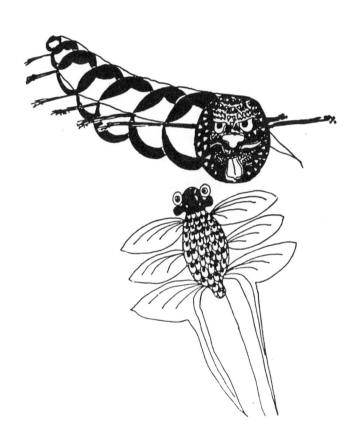

Table of Contents

A teachers' guide developed by Western Education Development Group

"I never can do it," the little kite said,
As he looked at the others high over his head;
"I know I should fall if I tried to fly."
"Try," said the big kite, "only try!..."

Mary Louise Friebele
The Little Kite

This book is dedicated to those free spirits who can still enjoy what many people consider child's play, kite flying. The resistance, I think, by adults to kite flying is either the result of past failures at kiting or the fear of drawing another adult's scorn. It is strange that no matter where I fly kites, people always stop to talk and ask questions.

One of the most important questions often asked of me is "Why won't my kite fly?" The question should be restated. "What do I have to do so that my kite will fly?" I hope this book answers the latter question.

I would like to thank Dr. C. J. Anastasiou for his time, advice and assistance in having this book published. A special thank you to Wendy Stockstad for her drawings, her patience on the many changes, and the cover graphics; thank you to Brenda Hyde and Selma Hammermeister for preparing the manuscript for publication, and to the Vancouver School Board for the time to piece the final draft together.

Frank Heyman

KIDS, KITES AND KINDERGARTEN

Almost any piece of paper will fly as a kite for children, provided the paper is strong enough for the job you want it to do.

This kite unit is for teachers of very small children who want to do a little extra to brighten a windy day.

First, make one of the enclosed or included kite plans into the real thing yourself and fly it. As you know, there is nothing like an enthusiastic instructor encouraging children, particularly one who has experienced the pleasure of success in flying a kite.

Begin with the *Chiringa,* a kite from the sunny land of California. This high-flyer needs no frame other than the folds in the paper which give the *Chiringa* its ability to fly.

Included here for your enjoyment is a photocopy master. Try it—you'll have instant fun with this one. Just photocopy and follow the step-by-step instructions to a flying good time.

Start with a square piece of paper or the included plan, if you wish, then fold the kite following the letters.

My kite classes have had equal success with any of the following materials:

- 18 x 18 cm rainbow coloured construction paper,
- three-hole punched lined loose-leaf paper,
- plastic mylar used for overhead projector transparencies,
- aluminum foil, etc.

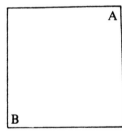

Fold A to B

A to B will give you your first crease—make it sharp by pulling your fingernails along the fold.

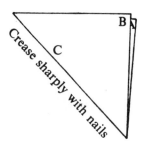

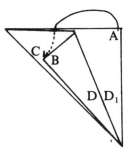

Fold A and B back, on the outside, to the crease at C. A and B are now folded back up to D and D₁.

After you have completed these folds and sharpened the creases, the Chiringa's basic shape is set.

The folding should take not more than two or three minutes at the most. The last fold is the only place where younger children will have difficulty. It is easy for the children to fold the final wing incorrectly if they do not follow instructions. If they don't fold it correctly, the kite won't fly.

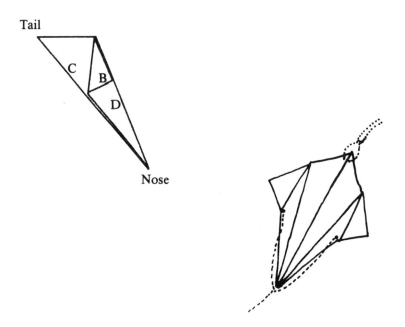

Now add the bridle. Any means of poking a small hole in the crease of the outside fold will do, a sharpened pencil, a ball point pen, nails all work equally well. Poke this hole about 1 cm to 1½ cm from the edge of the paper. Cut about 45 cm of thread, lay an end over a hole and push it through the hole with your pencil point. Tie a large loose loop. Use a reef (square) knot. It does the best job and doesn't slip. Poke the other end through the other hole and tie. A tapestry needle with thread does the most accurate job but your pencil point will do. Make the hole as close as possible to the lead edge. Gummed reinforcements glued right up to the edge work well but are not necessary.

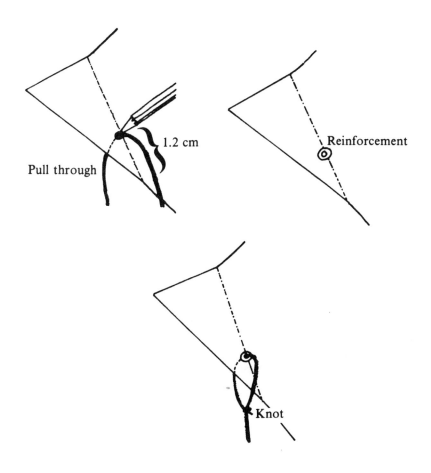

Pull through

1.2 cm

Reinforcement

Knot

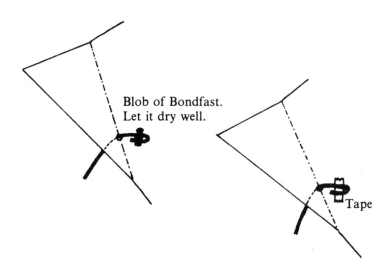

Blob of Bondfast.
Let it dry well.

Tape

If some children have trouble tying knots, the bridle can be attached with glue, gummed rings, bits of sticky tape or anything else that will keep the thread from pulling back out the holes. A simple fold in the glued thread will help.

3

The bridle is attached to both small wings in a loop and should be just long enough for the nose to pass through. If your bridle string is too long this can be corrected by knotting the loop at the nose. This little loop makes an excellent attachment point for your flying line. Tear or cut about 1½ cm off the nose. This tidies up the small tears which seem to come with folding.

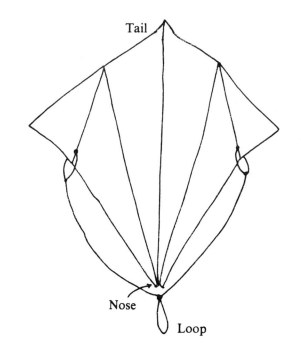

Tail

Nose

Loop

1. These ends are attached to the kite.

2.

Over and under and through the loop.

3.

Loop formed.

To find the center of the bridle for your kite, hang the Chiringa on a pencil, center it and tie your little loop. If the two legs are not even, the flight will be erratic.

To construct the tail, poke a hole through both sides of the kite at the tail end and push your thread through. Tie and knot another large loop. Use at least a half metre of thread. If you don't leave a lot of thread for the tail, it sometimes twists, knots and pinches your kite, leaving you with a tangled wreck in seconds.

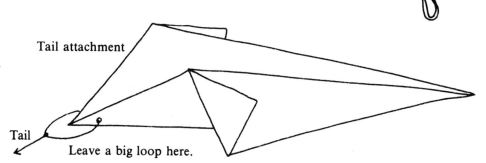

Tail attachment

Tail

Leave a big loop here.

4

For the tail, a party streamer will give you colour and plenty of length. Crepe paper cut across the folds works equally well and gives a riotous range of colours. Be generous—use two different coloured two metre streamers. You can always tear a little off if the tail is too heavy.

This little kite is my fun kite to start classes on. Everyone constructs one kite. Then, as a class, we head for an open space, spread out, put our backs to the wind, stand perfectly still and launch the Chiringas directly to the wind from our hands. A mass flying by the whole class is a wild, colourful and breathtaking experience. All the different colours, the excitement of the children's voices and a bright spring day have never failed to thrill me.

The launch can be carried out more smoothly by making sure the children are not standing too close to one another; that they hold their kites until they are at the specified launch area; and that they do not run where a group is flying kites. (Running inevitably produces tangled kite strings.)

One tip for easy launching is to gently push the center crease away from the bridle for flying position. This crease will usually "pop" once airborne, but just in case it doesn't, this little precaution will help the novice to become airborne immediately.

I am sure Chiringas can be made out of anything that will hold a crease. Try a new material. We flew a Chiringa out to the end of five hundred metres of fine silk thread before we lost it when the line broke. Maybe your class can beat this "record". At Qualicum Beach, we "sailed" two Chiringas at the end of 150 m of thread out into Georgia Strait. The bottom end of the thread was tied to a short stick which dragged across the waves. We watched until they passed out of sight, heading North towards Fanny Bay.

WHEN TO FLY?

The best time to fly your kite is after lunch. Morning winds are too rolly and tend to toss kites rather violently. Stay away from buildings as they make rolly winds too.

As a weather study, tell the children the type of day you would like to have for flying. They will watch and observe very keenly on their own. Introduce cloud types, highs and lows, precipitation, barometric readings. You will get a very pleasant surprise at the development and use of a weather vocabulary between the children. When the *right* day arrives, they will tell you.

Morning winds roll and gust.

Afternoon winds are steadier.

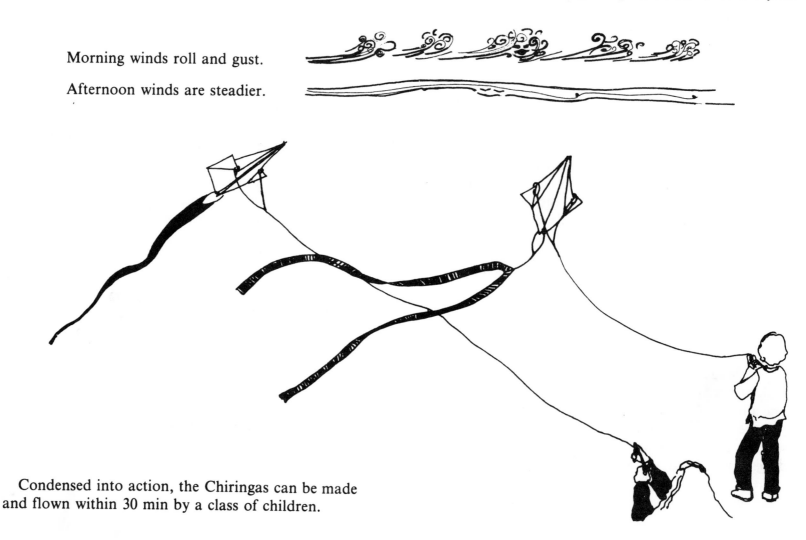

Condensed into action, the Chiringas can be made and flown within 30 min by a class of children.

YOUR FIRST KITE

Fold A to B and crease very sharply.
Fold A to B to C (C as on the back).
Then fold A back to D and B back to D_1.

The two X's are for the bridle attachments—reinforce with gummed rings or a small piece of scotch tape.
This kite is like the Bumblebee. No one believes that it will fly until they see it in the air.
Use this page for a Spirit Master maker for your copy machine and give all the children a kite to start with.
Just use your duplicating paper for the kite, it works beautifully.
For added excitement have your children do their own plan on paper—use *metrics* for measuring.

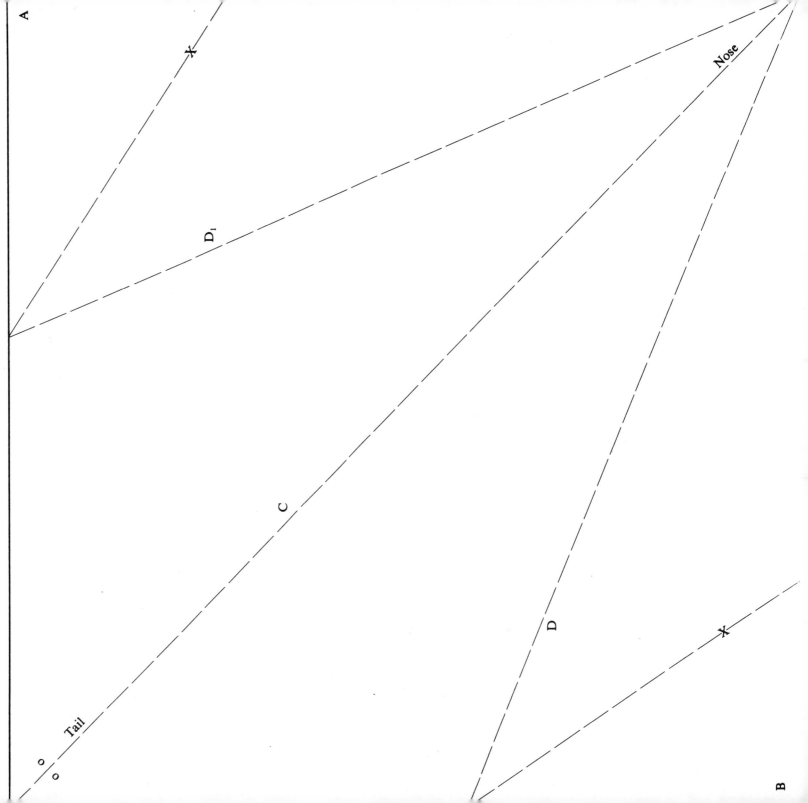

THE SAUSAGE BALLOON KITE

A long sausage shaped balloon for each child will get you started on this kite. Try this kite as a quick, one lesson kite to build and fly on a sunny afternoon. Have extra balloons on hand in case of breakage, two or three airmattress foot pumps to save small cheeks, two or three rolls of 1 cm masking tape, light card stock or heavy construction paper, and a lot of thread.

Blow your balloons up and knot the end. Cut a wing shape from your card stock. If you use construction paper, fold it in half and use the crease for your leading edge. You need the double thickness to keep the paper from folding out of the wing shape.

1.

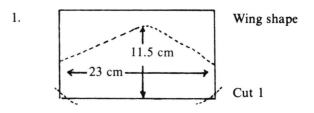

2.

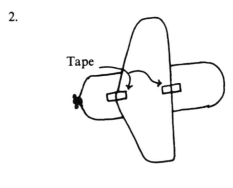

3.

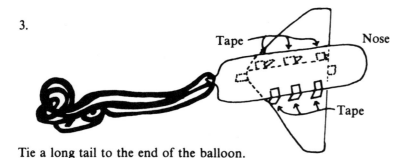

Tie a long tail to the end of the balloon.

4.

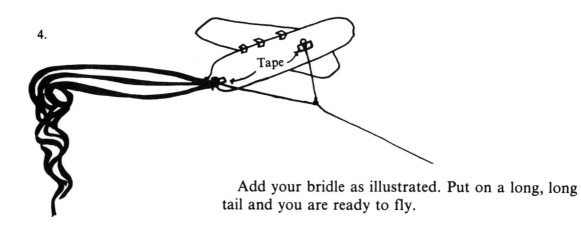

Add your bridle as illustrated. Put on a long, long tail and you are ready to fly.

Template for Balloon Wing

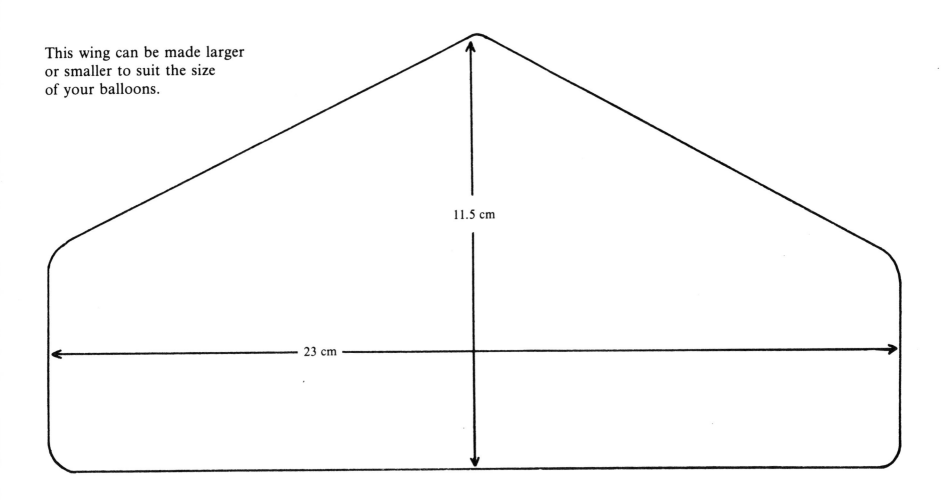

This wing can be made larger or smaller to suit the size of your balloons.

11.5 cm

23 cm

THE LITTLE SQUARE FLAT KITE

This kite is also very easy to construct and fly. The keys for making this one fly are (a) the bridle
(b) the tail
(c) the teacher.

18 x 18 cm construction paper works very well. There are several ways of framing this kite, but confusion is kept to a minimum if you work step by step through one way only.

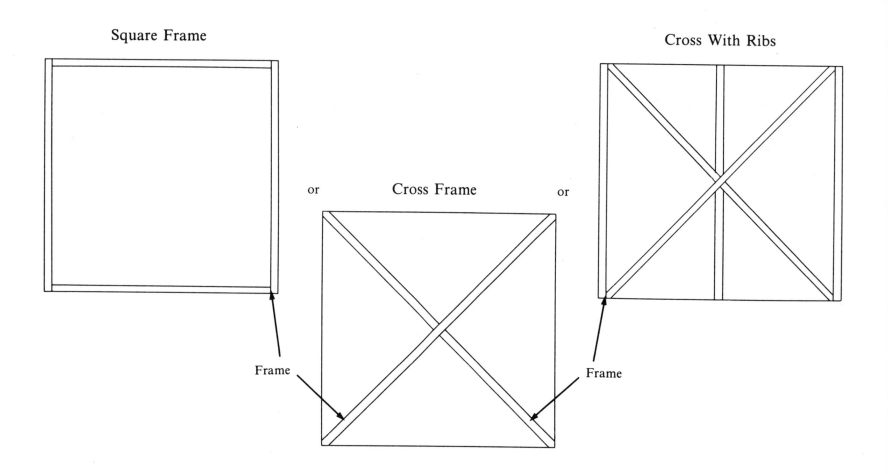

Square Frame

or   Cross Frame   or

Cross With Ribs

Frame   Frame

Caution   All young children develop the *too much*
syndrome

ENCOURAGE FRUGALITY WITH GLUE

To outline your kite, use anything that is light and strong, i.e., soda straws, bamboo skewers, split popsicle sticks, balsa wood, etc. Use the glue sparingly but use enough to do the job. Bondfast poured in small dabs on squares of wax paper, then applied by finger, is very satisfactory.

Bridle arrangements are as many as there are frame possibilities. The easiest bridle is one piece of string about 45 cm long and attached to the mid points at the top and bottom of the kite. A small loop should be tied on the bridle about 1/3 from the top (or 15 cm for front leg and 30 cm for the back leg). This bridle arrangement needs a long tail to balance the kite in the wind.

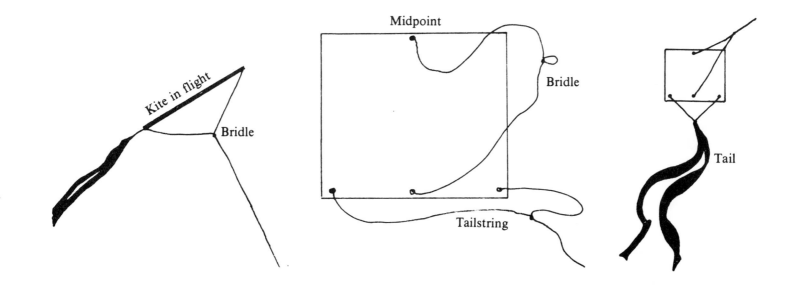

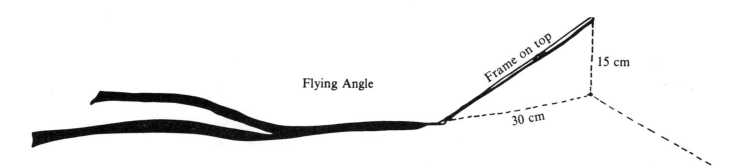

Flying Angle

Frame on top

15 cm

30 cm

A four corner harness is better, but little fingers have difficulty in finding a point where the strings should be knotted. Stay with the one string and a long colourful tail. Fly with the sticks on the top side of the kite. Here again a sharpened pencil or a tapestry needle is easiest for making holes and threading.

Don't be afraid to use a lot of crepe for tails, the extra material is worth the sight. Indian Cobra Kites with a face surface area of about 30 cm square have 4½ to 5½ m tails.

Glue the tail right to the kite.

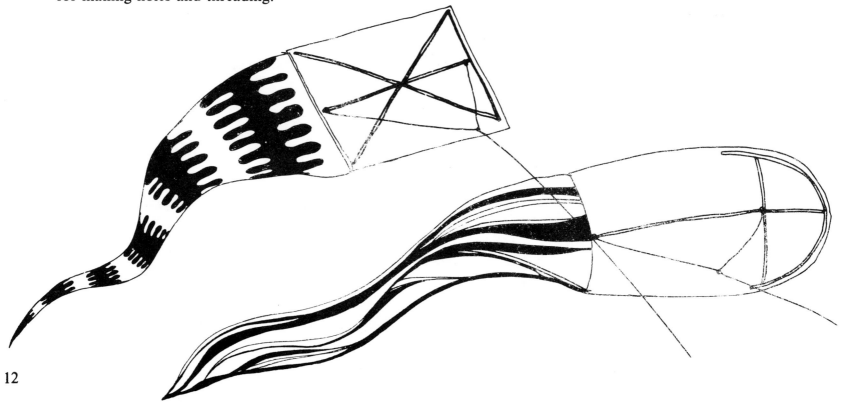

These kites and their variations will all fly if the rule of balance is followed.

When the kite is hung straight down it should lie flat in the air. If it twists to the bridle, the light side will have to be weighted. If weighting is impratical, have the children retie their kiteframes.

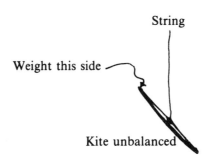

String

Weight this side

Kite unbalanced

String

Kite balanced

The frame or skeleton of the kite can be made either by gluing the individual pieces to the paper, or the shape desired can be made first and the paper glued on after. I find the first method works best when working with 18 x 18 cm construction paper or light card and the second when working with straws and tissue paper. (Illustrations on following pages.)

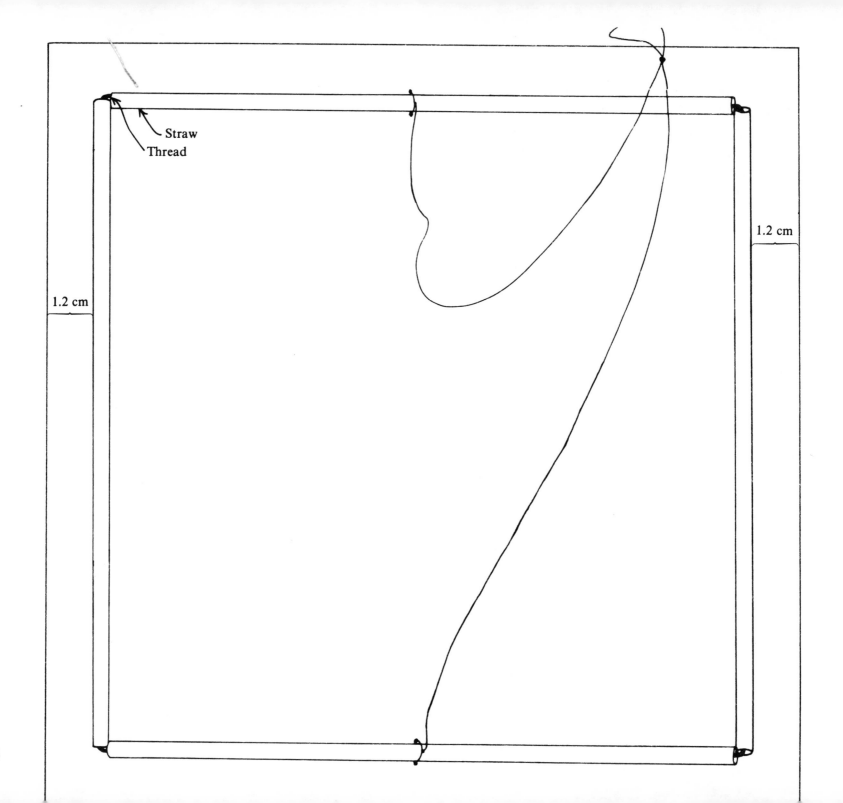

Straw

Thread

1.2 cm

1.2 cm

14

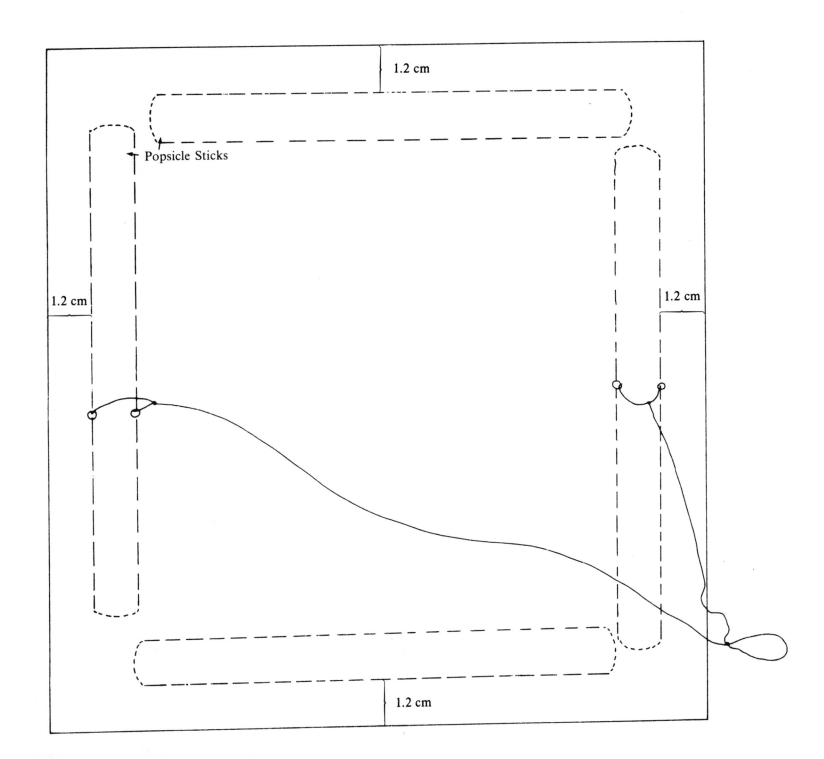

1.2 cm

Popsicle Sticks

1.2 cm

1.2 cm

1.2 cm

15

Straws, string and tissue paper are molded for strength and durability.

Make a square from 4 straws by threading them together and tying *tightly*. (Make 3 squares.)

Frame can be strengthened by inserting one straw inside the other and folding four corners.

Place your straw square on the tissue paper and cut the paper 3 to 5 cm larger.

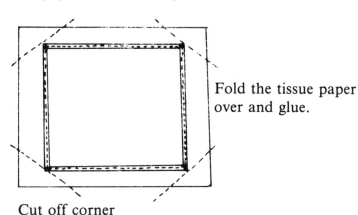

Fold the tissue paper over and glue.

Cut off corner for neatness.

For an eye-pleasing variation of the flat kite, try tying and flying 3 squares together.

When your 3 squares are completed, tie together and decorate. Add a large long tail for balance. This kite flies best in a good steady wind.

THE TRUSTY TWO STICKER — THE EDDY BOW KITE

This kite is guaranteed to fly. Follow the instructions plus a few simple rules and you're in the High-flyer group.

Making the Frame:

The usual practice is to notch the ends of the two sticks to provide a groove to run the outlining string around; this requires a small saw and time. For my classes thumbtacks are used, one pushed in at each end and the framing string is wound once or twice, then the tack is pushed in tight. This speeds the frame making considerably. One tip recently shown me by a local kite flyer is to staple a square piece of cardboard on to the frame to steady it for tying and at the same time hold your 90 degree angles at the cross point.

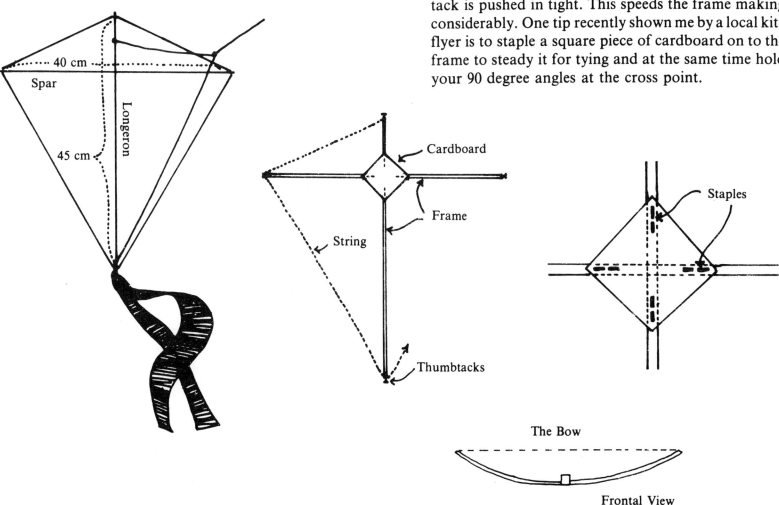

40 cm

Spar

Longeron

45 cm

Cardboard

Frame

String

Thumbtacks

Staples

The Bow

Frontal View

17

When the frame has been strung and securely tied, the cardboard can be removed and the covering material applied.

Tie the cross spar to the longeron about 13 to 15 cm from the top, then outline the frame with cord or heavy string and cover with whatever material is handy—newspaper is good (cheap and strong), plastic bags are excellent—but buy bright colours or clear plastic which can be felt-penned.

Lay your frame on the covering material, cut as shown. Flaps are folded over string and glued to secure your material.

The bridle knots (extra loops in flying line) can be changed to suit different wind conditions.

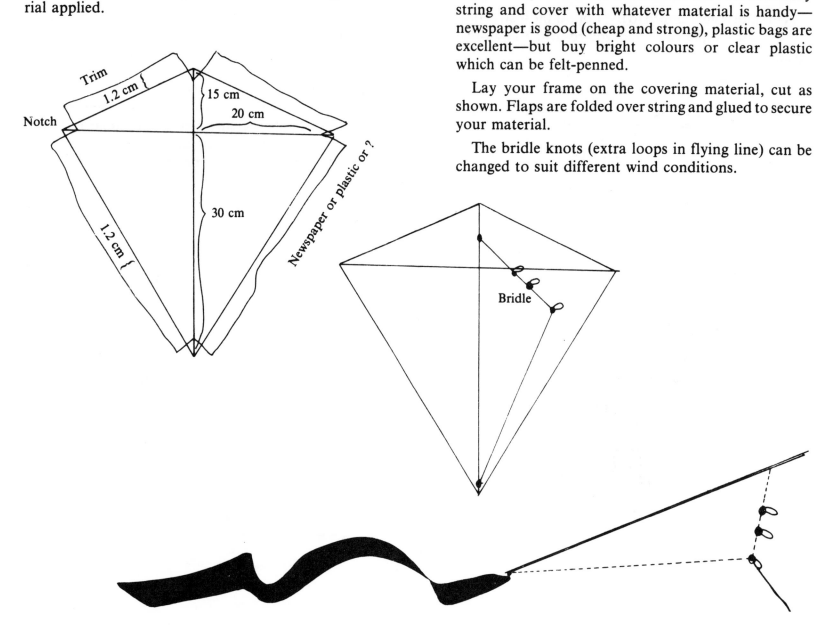

Please take extra time to impress upon the children the importance of balance. Care should be taken at all times to make sure one side is not too heavy. Balance your kite by adding the necessary weight (e.g. add a little glue, paper, or plasticene) to the light side—*do not trim weight away.*

Minor problems with balance will usually be corrected by the tail of your kite.

An easy way to check balance—

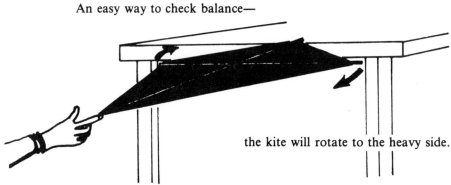

the kite will rotate to the heavy side.

Now that your kite is covered and balanced, the spar is ready for the bow. The spar is bent and the bow held by a string.

There are several ways to do this and every new class turns up a new idea.

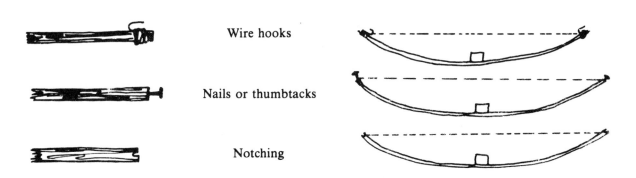

Wire hooks

Nails or thumbtacks

Notching

19

The bow string should be a few centimetres shorter than the spar to hold the bow. When the spar is bent, the loop is hooked over the nail and *voila,* a bow kite.

Nail

Loop

Here again, it's not how much weight you keep *off,* but how you use the weight you have. The lift from a kite 2½ m long will pull or jerk a good sized man off his feet and drag him along the ground. Several strung together will lift him right off the ground. The lift, then, of a small kite of the size you would build in class, say 1 m, will lift its own weight very easily even if you choose 2½ x 2½ cm wood and covered it with canvas. This kite built properly will fly without a tail, but since part of the fun of kites for children is a tail, make a long, light, colourful one.

Next time you make a trip to Chinatown, stop in at several of the novelty stores and look at the commercial kites from China.

20

They are quite heavy for their size—lots of bamboo, rice-paper, string, etc., but what long tails they have—all the better to fly them with. Many of the exotic kites—dragonflies, swallows, etc.—have a long string and paper tassles for their tails.

THE SCOTT SLED

This kite was patented by William Allison and is popularly called the Scott Sled. The sled is easy to construct and even easier to fly. The following designs are arranged from the smallest, for kindergarten, to largest, which would be a challenge for the older more able grade 3's.

The lunchbag kite can be cut out, taped, bridled and flown by grade 1's in about 30 mins. By using the sled pattern, this kite can be made from most any material available. If you do not wish to pleat and tape the sides as with the bags then you must use two stiffeners to give the kite lateral strength. Straws, rolled paper or balsa wood all work equally well.

Don't neglect the long bridle. It must be the 1 m length on the lunchbag (½ m for each leg), as this allows the kite to open properly and achieve its best flying characteristics. Tails should be long and light, attached either at the end of each stiffener or pleat or as a fringed skirt across the whole bottom of the kite.

The shape of the vent hole is not important. It can be square, circular, triangular or round. On calm days or for flying indoors, no vent is needed. Venting becomes necessary when wind conditions cause the sled to gyrate wildly.

LUNCH BAG SLED

Cut the bottom only from the bag, leaving an open sleeve. Draw the cutting pattern on the seam side of the bag and tape cutting pattern lines. Cut only the side of the bag that has the pattern and tape on it. Open the bag and tape the bottom face according to the pattern.

This will leave the sides of most bags as stiffeners on the top of the kite. Cut a 1 to 1½ m length of string for the bridle. Length of the bridle depends on the size of the bag. For smaller bags, do not use less than 1 m, otherwise the kite will not properly open for flying.

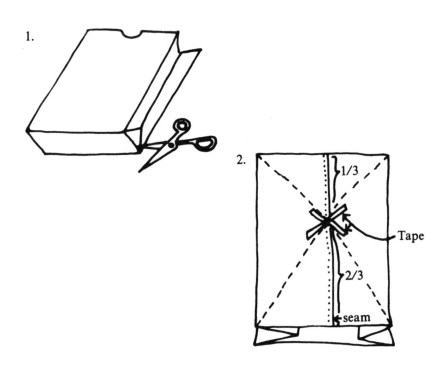

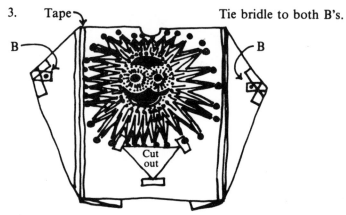

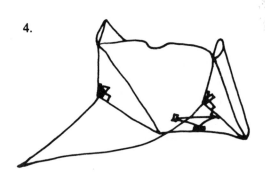

* Use a good quality light thread for bridling and flying this kite.

THE SCOTT SLED (MODIFIED)

This kite needs two sticks, dowels or rein-forced drinking straws, strong light paper or plastic garbage bags, string, appropriate tape and scissors.

Step I
Cut paper or plastic to size.

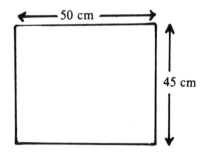

Step II
Fold in half. Cut out dotted pattern for *both sides*.

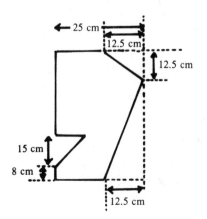

Step III
Open kite. Tape on longerons and attach bridle.

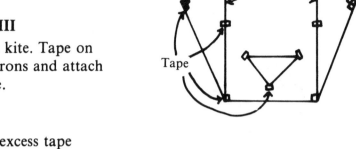

Fold excess tape over for double strength.

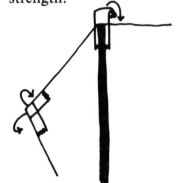

Bridle hole.

Poke with sharp point or pencil.

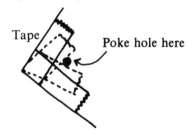

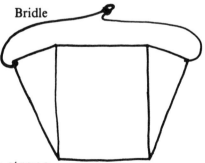

Bridle must be 1½ m to 2 m long for best performance.
(each leg ¾ to 1 m)

Cut a vent hole if wind is too strong.

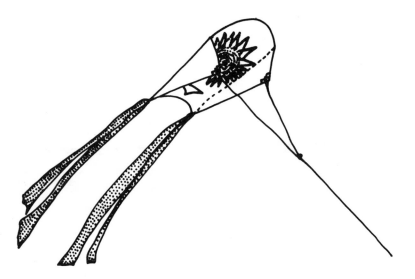

Add two long streamers to each longeron end for a beautiful eye-pleasing effect. You can fly this kite with no wind and a normal walking pace.

This kite can be made by cutting two plastic bags at the same time and taping the contrasting pieces together for a two colour sled.

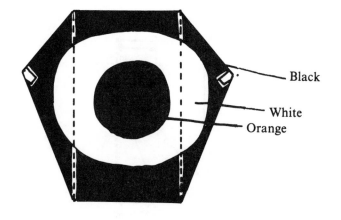

Black

White

Orange

LARGE SLED FOR A GROUP PROJECT

Recipe

1. Three bamboo garden stakes.
2. One large 75 cm x 125 cm plastic garbage bag.
3. A roll of plastic electrician tape.
4. Fishing line.
5. Eyelets and punch if you have one. (optional)

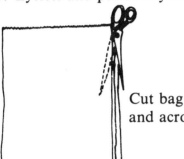

Cut bag open down one side and across the bottom.

Lay out flat and tape your bamboo on.

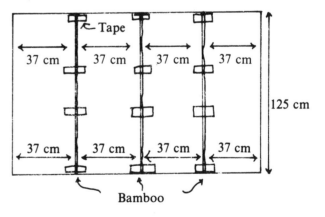

Tape

37 cm   37 cm   37 cm   37 cm

125 cm

37 cm   37 cm   37 cm   37 cm

Bamboo

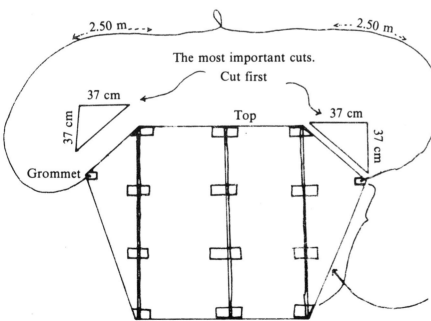

2.50 m   2.50 m

The most important cuts.

Cut first

37 cm

37 cm

Top

37 cm

37 cm

Grommet

Caution:

Cut the shape of the kite from the bag. Make sure the children realize that *if they cut the pattern incorrectly this kite will not work.*

* This cut is not critical, but should be as neat as possible.

25

CLASSROOM TIPS

Have all the material on hand before starting. For the Chiringa, have the paper, two pieces of string or thread for each child, pre-cut, pencils sharpened and any other materials that you might want—scissors, tape, gummed rings, etc. Follow step by step the folding directions—do not let the children rush ahead. Caution them that missed instructions just might make the difference between the kite flying or not.

Teaching Tip:

Children love to help children. Take advantage of this quality when kite building. The good knot tiers can help the slower ones. Missed instructions can be explained by students who have understood directions. Children who have completed their kites can help those who are having difficulty. Explain to the children that this co-operation will lead to the success of all kites and everyone will go outdoors together. This prevents slower students from giving up or losing interest and gives the faster students a chance to use their knowledge and skill to help others.

LAUNCHING FOR ALL KITES

Two good rules to observe:

(1) Don't run.

(2) When in doubt, don't pull.

Two methods for launching:

(1) The hand launch: put your back to the wind, hold your kite by the bridle attachment for the flying line and when the wind catches your kite, let it go. Release your line under tension, that is, you should always feel a pull as your kite rises. If you release too much line all at once, your kite may crash. As the kite rises and finds stronger steadier winds, let your line run out faster.

(2) With a partner: have a partner hold your kite 8 to 15 m downwind with its nose up. Call for a release and pull your line down and in. This will give height very fast. Once airborne, release your line as you would for the hand launch.

SAFETY TIPS

Spread the children out for flying room. This keeps tangles to a minimum. Keep any movement to a minimum—all kites can be launched from a standing position if the wind is right. Running just causes grief. An hour's work can be destroyed by not watching your kite during the launch.

Running creates two problems for the kites. You cannot see your kite if you are looking in the direction you are running. You might snag your kite or crash it or just drag it to pieces on the ground before realizing that something is wrong. Running backwards, obstacles you can't see create the problems. You may step on someone else's kite or tangle lines. Therefore avoid as much movement as possible during launching.

Trees are the bane of kiters. If you should be unfortunte enough to tangle with a tree, don't pull. The easiest way to free a kite that has landed (?) on a tree is to let out kite line quickly. This will allow the wind to catch the kite and pull it free. If it is caught but flying free, walk as close to the tree as possible and break your line. The kite will usually pull the line through the tree, if it is not too tangled. With the tension of holding gone it will flutter to the ground on the other side. If the kite doesn't pull free, leave it and build another. A fall and broken bones are not worth the few cents it takes to build a new kite. Treat all snagged kites the same way, whether it be T.V. aerials, telephone poles, etc. Pulling the kite towards the obstacle it is caught on only creates violent motions which will tangle or ruin a kite that otherwise might be saved.

Caution

Never fly your kite in the vicinity of powerlines. But if your kite does tangle in powerlines, drop your cord immediately. Under no circumstances should there be any attempt to retrieve a kite tangled in wires. Only grief can result, either by a bad fall through climbing or by an electric shock, particularly if the kite is wet. Wet flying line is an excellent conductor of electricity to the ground, as are poles and other gadgets that might be used to free a kite. Do not pull on a kite to retrieve it from powerline tangles. You may cut through the insulation to the live wire or pull two wires together and blackout the neighbourhood. T.V. aerials are also a hazard. There is a danger in pulling older ones down. Permit no wire flying lines or lines with metal centers. Remember, grown-ups as well as children have been killed trying to free a kite from powerlines.

FLYING TIPS

Flying a kite is like fishing. When the wind "catches" the kite, anything can happen and playing the kite becomes important. Pulling on the string as the kite rises will cause rapid climbing. An exception: be careful if the kite's nose is pointing down—a pull on the line will cause a power dive and possibly a crash! To gain height, pull on the line to make the kite rise, pay out string fast as the kite floats away with the wind, pull on the string to make the kite climb again, and repeat the process until the kite will not hold any more line.

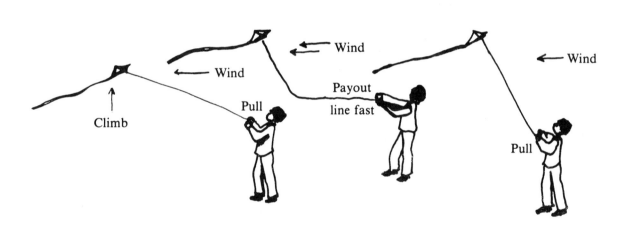

Climb

← Wind

Pull

← Wind

Payout
line fast

← Wind

Pull

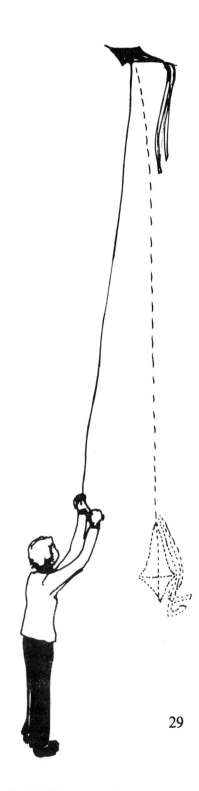

Power dives close to the ground are invitations for instant disaster. These start when your kite noses over and heads towards the ground. Crashes can be prevented by simply releasing several feet of string as quickly as possible. This removes the tension from the flying line, making a recovery possible. With the tension gone the kite should turn its nose back skywards and regain flying tension by itself. Don't pull your line—that only helps the wind and gravity speed your kite to a quick crash.

29

Corkscrewing is caused by either not enough tail for the wind condition or by poor balance or loss of balance when flying. If you have just launched your kite or it is close to the ground, relax the line tension immediately, release a lot of extra line and your kite should float gently to the ground. Check your balance, add more tail or make any necessary adjustments and repairs, then launch again.

Once the kite is airborne, playing the line by tensing and relaxing the string can give loop the loops, figure 8's, power dives, and so on. A rather spectacular stall can be obtained by flying the kite directly overhead, (90 degrees) and having the kite lose its lift. At this point the kite will nose over and fall like a leaf. Pulling the line will make the kite recover and the stunt can be repeated.

RETRIEVING SMALL KITES

The easiest and fastest way for young children to bring their kites down is to have a partner hold their reel, then place an arm over the flying line and run along the line until the kite is in hand. If the flying field is not long enough to permit this, walk the line as far as you can, then go back to your starting point (with your line in hand) and repeat the exercise until the kite is down and all the line is wound back onto the reel. This recovery is fast and prevents the procrastinators from being late at recess or noon.

For small children, use a heavy cardboard tube which their arm can go through for line. It is a cheap and easily made reel. Most furniture stores are only too happy to give these carpet tubes to teachers. If requested, most children can find something adequate to wind line on.

Cardboard tube

Coffee can

Centre post

HOW TO GET STARTED

By now you should be thoroughly convinced that kite flying can be a lot of fun. How do you get started? One way might be to send your children on a scavenger hunt, give them a list of desired materials: bamboo poles and stakes, one old cedar fence post, bamboo window shades, thread, and anything else you feel is "collectable" for your kites.

Push all your desks to the corners of the room and work on the floor. Make sure the children *all* have basic supplies—sticks, covering materials, scissors, string, tape, etc. Then arrange a central pool of materials in the center of the room where extra supplies can be obtained when needed and to which the excess can be returned.

Discourage the carrying of scissors in the classroom by hanging rolls of tape and scissors from chalkboards for easy access. Extra lengths of tape can be pre-cut and hung on desks for those who run short. Have the children hang this tape from desks near their work area; this stops long lineups at the dispenser. The children can cut needed lengths immediately from their own personal supply. This technique is perhaps the best way to handle plastic tape.

After giving instructions, let the children work uninterrupted until they are all finished that specific step. Encourage the children to help one another in actual construction and have *them* relate missed instructions to ones who don't listen or are confused. This will prevent "instant" lineups in front of you for instructions. You will now have time to walk around and help children who are working but are having trouble. Explain to the children that this is the only way that everyone will be ready to fly at the same time. This bears a good deal of repetition for it to sink in to some students—it is also useful in other subject areas, as you well know. If you feel that a demonstration is necessary first, do it quickly, otherwise the fidgeting starts and the whole point of the exercise will be lost. The children love the hands-on of the actual construction, therefore why not use your energy along with the class.

CREATIVE COVERINGS

Why not combine kite flying with your art lessons to produce unique kite coverings? Here are a few suggested techniques which work very well with paper and cloth. Some will even work with plastic.

(1) Block printing using: potatoes or carrots, wood, plasticine, styrofoam
(2) "Resists" using: masking tape, sticky tape or homemade paste
(3) Tie dying
(4) Batiking
(5) Water Colouring
(6) Silk Screening
(7) Posters
(8) Collages
(9) Newspaper and Spray Paint
(10) Stencils
(11) Splatter Painting
(12) String Painting
(13) Marbling with old cans of enamel paint

Your kite is capable of amazing lifting feats, therefore make it a work of art as well as a practical experience in flying. Add fringes, streamers and tails wherever possible for eye appeal. Try these following techniques along with many various art materials available.

Block printing by carving a pattern in any of the materials suggested in (1) above, and then stamping a repeated design will produce eye-pleasing effects in colour. Use soft materials that the children can cut and carve with kitchen knives (saves bandaids and fingers).

"Resists" work very well. Have the children use some of those old rolls of brown packaging tape that pile up in stockrooms (the brown kind used in butcher shops that has to be wet) or masking tape if you can afford it. Stick slightly to your material and spray, spatter or brush on your colours. When dry, lift the tape and your design appears.

For cloth and brush dyeing, a paste resist can be made very easily by adding one cup of flour very slowly to one cup of water. You may have to add a little more flour to thicken your mixture, but not too much. Stir until smooth; dry lumps may cause weak spots in your resists, but then, that may be an added bonus. Apply your resist with plastic squeeze bottles. Then paint the areas of your designs with Rit permanent dyes. To fix your colours and remove the resist, wash in lots of warm soapy water. This should cause little if any colour blending and give you bold colours outlined in white. This resist should be completed the same day to avoid deterioration of the dyes.

Tie dying (cloth or paper)—Cloth should be dyed with permanent colours for lasting effects. Paper, on the other hand, can be dyed with food colouring. Coverings for small kites can be made from triple thick man-sized Kleenex tissue. Tissue paper and rice paper also lend themselves very nicely to this technique. Fold your paper into squares, triangles, or pleats and dip the corners and edges into different colours, put drops of colour on open areas. Open paper while still wet and press between newspaper to dry. Iron when dry to remove wrinkles.

Batiking can be carried on at a very simple level on paper or cloth by the following means. Using melted parafin wax (use an electric frypan, the safest method if you don't have a proper wax melter), apply your wax by brush or small juice can depending on the desired pattern. Remove your wax by using a hot iron. If you place your material between a sandwich of paper towels and newspaper, the ironing will melt the wax and it will be absorbed by the paper towels. If you don't want to wax-up a frying pan, melt your wax in small cans set into hot water in the frying pan. (**Caution:** Don't give children open access to the pan.)

Brush your colours on between wax applications. *Tip*—start with lightest colours first and work up to dark colours. Food colouring will give you brilliant designs on paper.

Water colours—the traditional method of painting Japanese kites. Let your imagination go here; Silk Span and Rice Paper will take water colours very nicely and will shrink slightly as the paint dries. This will give you a very tight lifting surface for flat kites and a bonus in flying stability. Paint this paper after you have applied it to the kite frame.

Silk Screening can be a lot of fun but care must be taken not to rush. Make small frames from 2 to 3 cm wood. Explain to the children they will need a frame for each colour they plan to use, therefore limit their colours to a reasonable number.

Wood

Old posters with their bold colours and scenes could be used. Choose the best part of the scene and you have an "instant" decoration.

Kite collages of coloured tissue paper can be made with fringe everywhere. A kite of eyes, lips, noses—the childrens' imaginations will produce endless ideas based on collages.

Stencils are another way of achieving beautiful design with a simple technique. Cut your design or pattern from cardboard or tag and spatter paint, spray or paint with a brush.

String painting—Dip several feet of string into desired colours and then, holding both ends, draw them across the covering to make a feathered effect or just drop, curl and snake the string to produce a design.

Marbling—Have the children bring small cans of leftover enamel paint. Place a lot of newspaper around where you plan to do this. Use a large enamel photographer's developing pan (easily cleaned) or a large cookie pan (which can be kept for this purpose since the paint won't easily come off it). Fill the pan with water then splatter large drops of enamel paint on to the surface of the water. Colour blending and patterns can be developed by combining the floating colours with cotton swabs. Carefully roll the paper onto the surface of the water until it is flat. This will force all the air out from between water and paper and when you lift the paper the paint will be stuck in a beautiful pattern. Since it will be heavy, use this paper on kites for heavy winds.

TROUBLES FROM LAUNCHING TO FLYING TO LANDING

Cautions:

(1) Stay away from buildings, trees and other obstacles. Winds are extremely turbulent downwind. You might launch your kite there, but a class of children will produce a disaster.

(2) If your kite is not flying as it should, check the *Things to watch for.*

(3) When landing a kite, try to bring it right to hand without having it strike the ground. This prevents broken pieces and ripped covers. Some kites just do not want to land without attempting to dash themselves to pieces. If this is the case with your kite, try to land it using a lot of slack line. That is, when you have it in a position where you can land it on the field without tangling with obstacles such as trees, backstops, people, etc., release enough line fast to let the kite "float" on the wind, then by tensing your line and releasing slack, you can bring your kite in for a smooth landing. If possible have a helper to take the kite in hand *after* it touches down. This prevents sudden take-offs as you hold the line and walk down it to retrieve your kite.

THINGS TO WATCH FOR

Bridle—for your kite to fly properly under all conditions, the bridle may have to be adjustd to suit wind conditions. The lighter the wind, the more critical the angle of attack to the wind, therefore shorten the front bridle string as wind speed increases.

Balance—a tendency to dive to one side or the other consistently. Check for loose fittings, knots, etc.

Tail—the stronger the wind, the more tail is needed. Add a plastic cup (punch out the bottom). Use a paper parachute, small plastic bags with holes, or just make your tail longer if it is a streamer.

Power Dives, Looping, Uncontrollable Gyrations— Check for loose fittings and tears, particularly sleds made from plastic; at times the longerons come untaped or slip, causing loss of balance. Check bridles for short legs, loose knots or slipped knots.

Nose Dives—release a lot of line immediately. This will cause the kite to "float" with the wind and turn its nose up. When the nose is up, pull down hard on the kite string and your kite will climb out of danger.

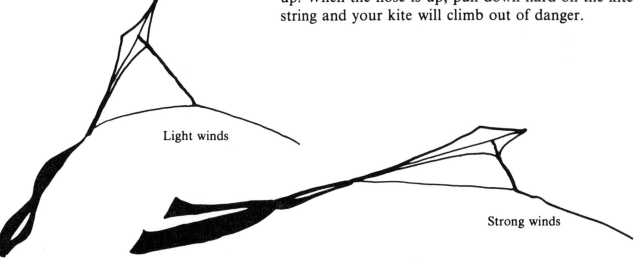

Light winds

Strong winds

BEAUFORT SCALE OF WIND FORCE ON LAND

Indications	Miles per Hour	Description
Leaves still	Less than 1	light
Slight rustle of leaves	1 - 3	light
Wind felt on face Vane moved by wind	4 - 7	gentle
Leaves and twigs in constant motion	8 - 12	gentle
Raises dust and small papers Moves small branches	13 - 18	moderate
Small trees sway	19 - 24	fresh
Large branches in motion Whistling in wires Umbrellas used with difficulty	25 - 31	strong
While trees in motion	32 - 38	strong
Breaks twigs off trees	39 - 46	strong
Slight damage to buildings	47 - 54	gale
Seldom experienced Trees uprooted	55 - 63	whole gale
Very rare Much damage	64 - 75	whole gale
	above 75	hurricane

SUITABLE WIND SPEEDS FOR DIFFERENT KITE TYPES

	No Breeze	0 - 5	6 - 10	11 - 15 gloves helpful	16 - 20 use gloves	21 - 30 use gloves	30 and up	Adaptability to Changes in Size
			Miles Per Hour					
Chiringa	X	X	X					very little
Sleds	X	X	X	X	X	X		excellent
Rectangular Japanese	X	X	X	X	X	X		good
Two Stick Flat Kite	X	X	X					good
Eddy Bow	X	X	X	X	X	X		excellent
Stub Nose Kite (Bermuda)	X	X	X					good
Box (Basic)	X	X	X	X	X	X		excellent
Basic Parawing	X	X	X					good
Winged Box			X	X	X	X		excellent
Delta Kite (Bat)		X	X	X	X			excellent
Parafoil		X	X	X	X		If you do any kite flying in this weather, count your children before and after flying.	difficult to make smaller
Hexagonal Three Stick	X	X	X					good
Triangular Box			X	X	X	X		excellent
Oriental Kites	X	X	X					good
India Fighter	X	X	X					excellent
Parawing	X	X	X					good

These are approximate values for flying conditions.

One rule of thumb: the stronger the wind, the bigger the kite and the longer the tail.

SOME MORE DIFFICULT KITES

The Rectangular Japanese Kite
Material Recipe

2 sticks 53 cm for the cross
1 stick 44 cm for a keel
1 stick 36 cm for the bow

(Approximate
Measurements)

Fold over flap and glue.

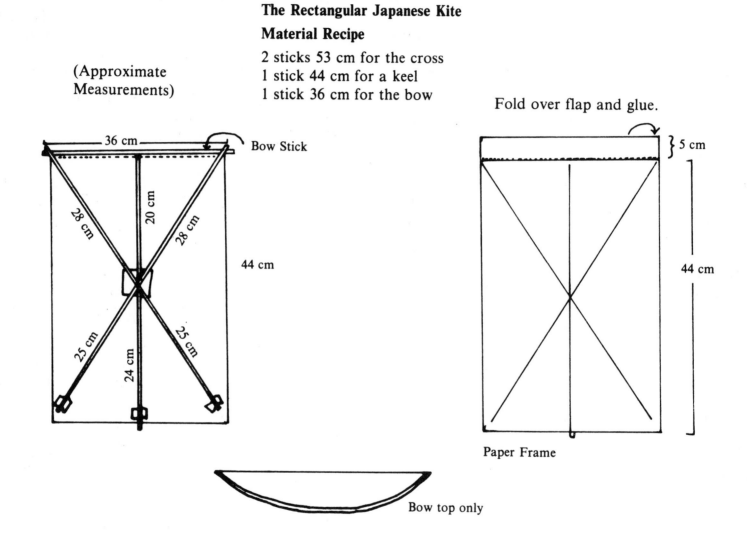

36 cm — Bow Stick

20 cm

28 cm

28 cm

25 cm

25 cm

24 cm

44 cm

5 cm

44 cm

Paper Frame

Bow top only

Use any material that is handy: heavy kraft wrapping paper, white wrapping paper, grocery bags, plastic, nylon film or what have you.

Make the basic frame including the bow stick. Tie all sticks with a little thread; one or two wraps is more than enough. Dab knots with white glue or Bondfast. Cut the paper to the size of the frame leaving a 1 cm flap to wrap over the bow stick for gluing. Apply glue to the frame and stick to paper, fold flap over bow and glue. Let the kite dry thoroughly and add a box string. This kite flies best with a two point bridle and a long (colourful) tail. This kite is a good stunt flyer. It also lends itself very well to changes in size, just keep your ratio as close as possible.

✖ ✖ ✖

Two Celled Kite

Here is a one stick kite that can be very quickly built using railroad board, sticky tape, two ½ cm thick elastic bands, scissors and string.

Use a strong spruce dowel or bamboo garden stake 70 cm long. Two pieces of light card or railroad board 20 x 89 cm. Score the cardboard 24 cm in from each end and fold on the score line. When folded, the cardboard will form a triangular cell. Tape with wide 6 cm masking tape or sticky tape. Reinforce if necessary as flying stress may cause the tape to pull off if it is the 2½ cm masking tape. Cut tape longer than the cells and fold the excess inside the cell. Make two cells.

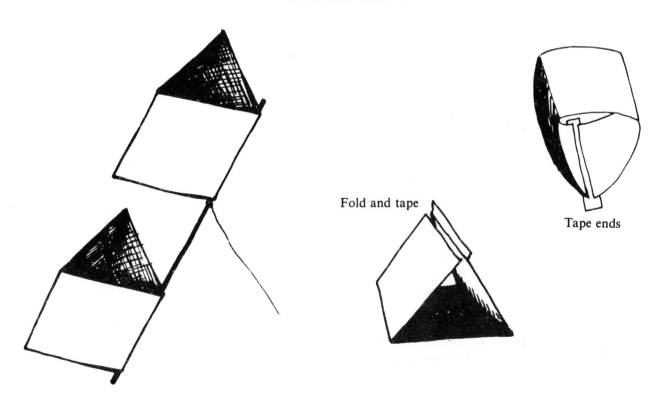

Fold and tape

Tape ends

Hang the two rubber bands on the stock towards the center of the longeron, now slip a cell over the end of the longeron. Twist the rubber band to cinch it on the longeron, stretch it to the outer end of the longeron, twist and loop over the end two or three times to ensure the cells do not fly off in flight. Repeat for second cell. Attach string next to one of the cells and it is ready to fly.

Stick

Elastics

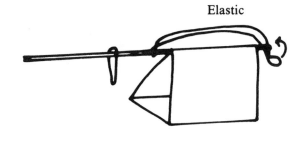

Elastic

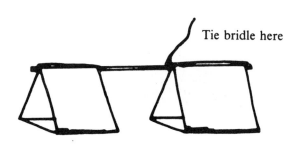

Tie bridle here

The Indian Fighter Kite

This kite also adapts very nicely to changes in size.

For framing, almost any light flexible material will do: bamboo, cedar, spruce, or reinforced drinking straws. You will also need thread, glue or sticky tape, and a fairly strong piece of paper for the covering and scissors.

Position the keel and glue to the paper leaving about 2½ cm of clearance from the bottom. This is then folded up and glued into place on the bottom of the keel.

The length of the bow stick should be the distance from the two wing tips.

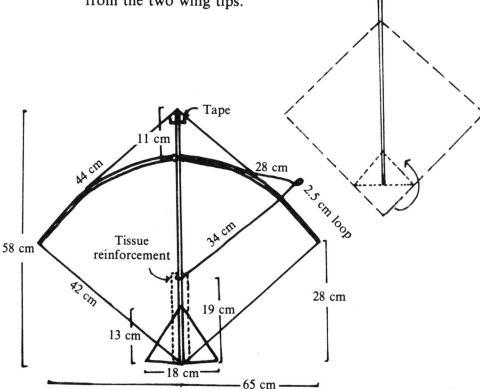

40

Using thread, bend the bow stick so that about 2½ cm clearance is left at the kite edge for folding and gluing the edges of the wings.

Once this basic shape is completed, glue strips of paper or tape from the frame to the flying surface.

This kite can be flown with very long tails giving it excellent flying stability, or with no tail for fighting. The tailless fighter is very difficult to fly, hence a need for a great deal of skill in flying. Wait for the nose to point in the direction you want it to go and pull hard. If it dives, release the line quickly—this will usually cause the fighter to nose-up, then, pull hard.

The bridle can have either one or two legs. Again, I prefer a two legged bridle for better control. For reinforced drinking straw frames, push one straw inside the other leaving about 1/3 of the first straw empty, then keep pushing straws into straws until the desired length is achieved. As the empty 1/3 of the first straw is cut off, take this into account when measuring your lengths.

Add a fin tail if you wish to fight this kite; light card stock will do for pleasure flying. Tie one long tail from the bottom of the longeron and a streamer from each of the wing tips. There are countless variations of this kite; it flys extremely well. Try a design of your own using this basic shape.

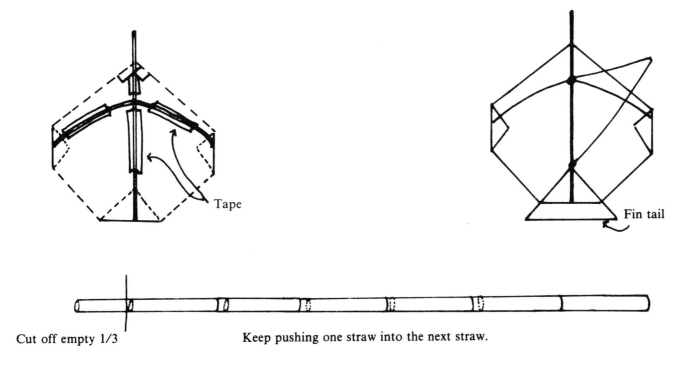

Tape

Fin tail

Cut off empty 1/3   Keep pushing one straw into the next straw.

Hexagonal or Bermuda Kite

This kite needs three sticks the same length and how you arrange them is up to you.

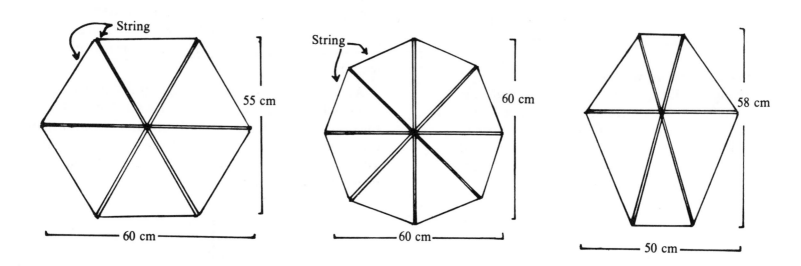

The covering can be a complete face or a broken face.
Four point bridles work best on this kite.

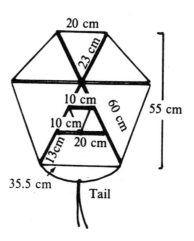

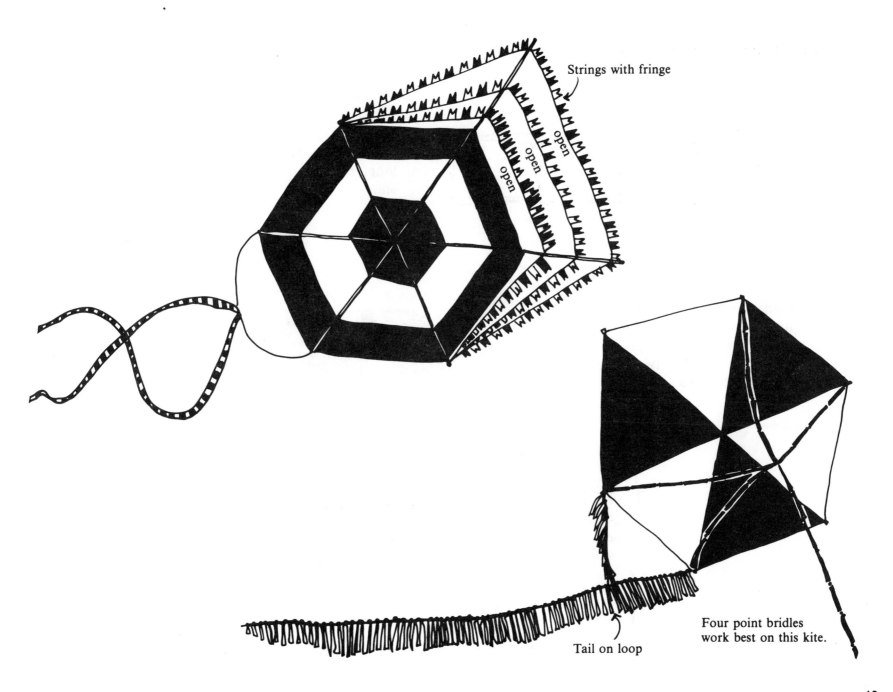

Strings with fringe

open
open
open

Tail on loop

Four point bridles
work best on this kite.

43

The Box Kite (Toothpick Version)

Make two

Make two sides three toothpicks long, blunt end glued to pointed end.

Stand sides between two supports and glue crosspieces on. Use glue sparingly, otherwise it takes too long to dry. The large blobs of glue tend to stay soft inside.

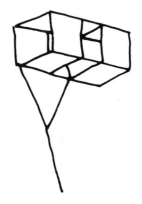

Tissue paper makes the most satisfactory cover and is colourful. Apply glue with your finger evenly over the toothpicks and apply your paper. Only the ends are covered, the middle cell is left open.

BIBLIOGRAPHY

Books

Barwell, Eve and Bailey, Conrad. *Making Kites.* London: Studio Vista, 1976. $1.00.
  A very good beginning book for children.
Brummit, Wyatt. *Kites.* New York: Western Publishing Company, 1971. (A Golden Handbook Guide) $3.00.
  A delightful thumbnail sketch of the history and personalities of kiting, profusely illustrated with lots of detailed kite plans.
Burkhart, Timothy. *Kite Folio.* London: Wildwood House; Berkley: Double Elephant, 1974. $5.00.
Carr, Ed. *Kites.* London: Macdonald Educational Ltd., 1979. $2.50.
  A must for a classroom kite project.
Consumer Guide. *Create-A-Kite.* New York: Simon and Schuster, 1977. $4.95.
  Excellent instructions and plans, very suitable for upper intermediate grades and high school.
Dyson, John and Dyson, Kate. *Fun with Kites.* London: Angus and Robertson, 1976. $5.00.
  18 beautiful kites, well illustrated, simple instructions.
Greger, Margaret. *Kites for Everyone.* Self-published, 1984. Margaret Greger, 1425 Marshall, Richland, WA 99352. $10.00.
  A super all-encompassing book on kites by a teacher for teachers.
Hunt, Leslie L. *Kite Making, Getting Started.* London: Collin-MacMillan. $2.95.
Jue, David F. *Chinese Kites: How to Make and Fly Them.* Tokyo: Charles E. Tuttle, 1972. $4.25.
  Excellent designs to challenge avid kitebuilders.
Mouvier, Jean Paul. *Kites.* Paris: Wm. Collins Sons and Co. $2.00.
  A must for beginners. All designs clearly illustrated, super for upper primary and intermediate grades.
Newnham, Jack. *Kites to Make and Fly.* Victoria: Penguin Books Australia, 1977. $1.25.
  A delightful book for kiteflyers and the classroom bookshelf.
Newman, Lee Scott and Newman, Jay Hartley. *Kite Craft.* New York: Crown Publishers, 1974. $10.00.
  A complete kite book. Suitable for teachers and library.
Pelham, David. *The Penguin Book of Kites.* Markham, Ontario: Penguin Books, 1976. $4.95.
  Good historical material. Some fine patterns, ample illustrations.
Streeter, Tal. *The Art of the Japanese Kite.* New York, Tokyo: Weatherhill, 1982. $12.00.
  Great for your library or teacher reference.
Wagenvoord, James. *Flying Kites.* Toronto: Collier-MacMillan Canada, 1968. $5.00.
  Instructions for building and flying 12 classic kite designs.

Periodicals

Kite Lines, 7106 Campfield Road, Baltimore, MD 21207. Four issues, U.S. $9.00. Magazine about kites and kiting around the world. A super book for libraries. Publishes reader input.
AKA News, 113 W. Franklin St., Baltimore, MD 21201. U.S. $15.00 annually. Bimonthly newsletter of the American Kitefliers Association.

Related Activities

Barnaby, Cap. Ralph S. *How to Make and Fly Paper Airplanes.* Toronto: Scholastic Book Services. 1972. $0.75.
Geary, Keith. *Make and Find Out.* London: MacMillan. 4 books, $1.00 each.
    Excellent resource for flying objects, planes and kites. However, most designs use European plastic containers.
Gibbs, Mike. *Parachutes.* Vancouver: VEEP, The University of British Columbia, 1975.
Mander, Jerry, Dipple, George and Gossage, Howard. *The Great International Paper Airplane Book.* New York: Simon and Schuster, 1967. $4.00.
Morris, Campbell. *Advanced Paper Aircraft Construction.* London: Angus & Robertson, 1984. $3.50.
    A super book.
Simon, Seymour. *The Paper Airplane Book.* New York: Viking Press. $0.65. (MacMillan in Canada.)
The Know How Book of Flying Models. London: Usborne Publishing, 1975.

KITE FLYING SAFETY CODE

This is the safety code of the International Kiteflyers Association.

As a member of the International Kiteflyers Association I will do my best to maintain the safety record of the organization and I will obey the safety code stated herein.

(1) I will obey the laws regarding local kite flying.
(2) I will not fly kites above the legal air limit set in my region.
(3) I will not fly kites across automobile roads.
(4) I will not fly kites in areas where there are power lines, nor will I try to recover kites that have become entangled in these lines.
(5) I will not fly kites which contain explosives of any kind.
(6) I will not fly kites on rainy days.
(7) I will not fly kites on beaches where there are a number of people present who may be cut by the strings.
(8) I will not fly razor blade studded kites.
(9) I will use gloves if flying kites five feet large or over.
(10) I will not fly kites in conditions of low visibility or in any area where they may endanger aircraft in flight.